An Evening with Yiayia

A Greek Grandmother's Gift of Stories and Poems

ANGELA VLACHOS RUTH
ILLUSTRATED BY LOUISE VAN WYK

Copyright © 2021 Angela Vlachos Ruth

All rights reserved under international
and Pan-American copyright conventions

Independently published in the United States
by Amazon Kindle Direct Publishing.

This book may not be reproduced, stored in a
retrieval system, or transmitted by any means
without the permission of the author.

Trademark permissions have been granted in writing.

ISBNs:
978-1-7364608-0-1 (Softcover)
978-1-7364608-1-8 (eBook)

First Edition

This book is dedicated to my grandson Nathan who brought out the very Greek Yiayia in me, and to my mother Diane who instilled a sense of Greekness to our home every day. She is small but she is mighty. We call her Little Big Yiayia.

Special thanks to Professor Ippokratis Kantzios, the Interim Department Chair of the University of South Florida's Department of World Languages who provided the gift of language and phonics editing to this work.

Note to Parents and Grandparents

Yiayia teaches the old Greek poem about children going off to a school by the light of the moon. It is interesting to note that historians have found that this secret school narrative emerged during the Greek Revolution of 1821. While some believe these stories are based on folklore, others believe secret schools truly existed during the restrictive years of the Ottoman empire, and that the Greek Orthodox Church strived to preserve its faith and the nation's language. What matters most to Yiayia is that this beautiful poem has been passed along from generation to generation for two centuries.

As far as the loukoumathes go - all cultures have fried dough recipes, and this is the Greeks' rendition. Loukoumathes are served at Greek festivals throughout the world, and can also be made at home easily with round balls of dough dipped in hot, hot oil and then soaked in honey and cinnamon! Or you may pick up fresh when visiting New York City at YiaYias Bakery or Omonia Cafe in Astoria, Queens.

For those of you looking for the Greek letter blocks, they can be found at Greekshops.com!

My yiayia is here!

Yiayia means grandmother in Greek.

My Yiayia is **very** Greek.

How Greek?
Well, as soon as she sees me,
she starts talking Greek!

Athanasios, Pos eisai simera?
(Πώς είσαι σήμερα)
means Athanasios,
how are you today?

S 'agapo toso poly
(Σ <αγαπώ τόσο πολύ)
means I love you so much!

As paixoume (Ας παίξουμε)
means Let's play!!

AND THEN...

We play

AND THEN...

Yiayia starts singing a song in Greek
that I have known since I was a baby!

Palamakia paixete
(Παλαμάκια παίξετε)
Kai i yiayia sou erchetai
(και η γιαγιά σου έρχεται)
Kai sou ferni kati ti
(και σου φέρνει κάτι τι)
Loukoumathes sto harti
(λουκουμαδες στο χαρτί!!)\

Translation:
Clap Your Hands!
Your Yiayia is coming,
and bringing you something!
What? Loukoumathes in
a paper wrapper!

AND THEN...

Yiayia's making me my favorite Greek dinner—skinny, buttery noodles called Fithes (φιδές) just like my daddy's Yiayia made for him!

I say "Nostimo" (νόστιμο)

which means

Delicious!!

And Yiayia was right—there's

Loukoumathes

for dessert!
AND THEN...

Yiayia teaches me history, about Greek children long ago who went to school at night by the light of the moon!

Fengaraki mou lambro
(Φεγγαράκι μου λαμπρό)
Fenge mou na perpato
(φέγγε μου να περπατώ)
Na piyeno sto skholio
(να πηγαίνω στο σχολειό),
Na matheno ghramata
(να μαθαίνω γράμματα),
Grammata spoudhamata
(Γράμματα σπουδάματα)
Too Thayoo ta pragmata
(του Θεού τα πράγματα.).

Yiayia tells me what it means:

My little shining moon,

Light my way so I can walk

To go to school,

To learn my lessons,

Reading and writing,

God's Wishes

Yiayia's yiayia taught her this poem.

AND THEN...

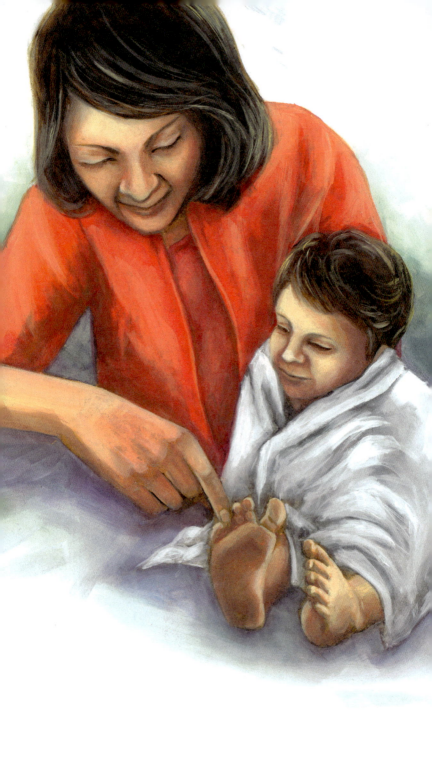

My Yiayia is silly.

She counts my toes to make sure they're all there!

Ena (Ενα) means one
Dio (Δύο) means two
Tria (Τρία) means three
Tes-se-ra (Τέσσερα) means four
Pen-de (Πέντε) means five
Exee (Εξι) means six
Ep-tah (Επτά) means seven
Och-toe (Οκτώ) means eight
En-n ay-ah (Εννέα) means nine
Theka (Δέκα) means ten

AND THEN...

I am ready for bed,

but first we say our prayers
which we call our prosefchi
(Προσευχή)
to ask God to watch over us,
our family,
and everybody in the
whole wide world.

Do you think I will dream about
my evening with Yiayia and all the
things she taught me? I do.

Kalinychta (καληνύχτα), Yiayia.

I say good night.
I am **very** Greek too.

AND THEN...

I fall asleep.

About the Author

A native of Chicago, Angela Vlachos Ruth is a wife, mother and yiayia. In her professional life, Angela served as the executive director of the Holland & Knight Charitable Foundation where she initiated a number of programs including Opening Doors for Children, the Holocaust Remembrance national essay contest as well as the creation of the New York Firefighters Memorial Wall.

Today, Angela continues to pursue her passion for education as an eighth grade history teacher at Carrollwood Day School. She is a graduate of the University of Tampa and received her masters degree in history at the University of South Florida.

Angela is the wife of a Pulitzer Prize recipient, and never believed she'd be the first to write a book in the family. As a mother she has always inspired her sons Philip and Alex to take pride in their Greek roots. The birth of her first grandchild, Nathan, inspired this book as a means of encouraging a love of Greek history and culture for the next generation.

About the Illustrator

Cape Town-based artist, Louise van Wyk, continuously expands her portfolio as she strives to master various paint techniques and mediums. This makes her extremely versatile and adaptable. Her incredible ability to translate emotion into visual art allows her to capture the most stripped down essence of beauty. This especially shows in her portraits and the way she captures the spirit of animals. Louise teaches art classes, working with adults in fun group settings and children, with a focus on learners with special educational needs. Her incredible talent as sketch artist has also created opportunities for her to do children's book illustrations. As an artist, her goal is simply to create beauty and to bring joy to anyone touched by her work. She has profiles on both Art Pal and South African Artists, where you can explore more of this multifaceted artist's work.

Made in the USA
Middletown, DE
08 April 2021